Make and Eat
Bread
& Pizza

Susannah Blake

WAYLAND

First published in 2008
by Wayland

Copyright © Wayland 2008

Wayland
338 Euston Road
London NW1 3BH

Wayland
Level 17/207 Kent Street
Sydney NSW 2000

Senior editor: Jennifer Schofield
Designer: Jane Hawkins
Photographer: Andy Crawford
Proofreader: Susie Brooks

Acknowledgements:
The author and publisher would like to thank the following
models: Adam Menditta, Jade Campbell, Aneesa Qureshi,
Taylor Fulton, Emel Augustin, Kaine Zachary Levy, Ammar
Duffus, Claire Shanahan.

All photographs by Andy Crawford except page 4:
Wayland Picture Library

CIP data
    Blake, Susannah
    Bread & pizza. - (Make & eat)
    1. Cookery (Bread) - Juvenile literature 2. Pizza -
    Juvenile literature 3. Baking - Juvenile literature
    I. Title
    641.8'15

ISBN: 978 0 7502 5355 0

Printed in China

Wayland is a division of Hachette Children's Books,
an Hachette Livre UK company.

Note to parents and teachers:
The recipes in this book are intended
to be made by children. However, we
recommend adult supervision at all times,
especially when using kitchen equipment,
as the Publisher cannot be held
responsible for any injury.

Contents

All about bread and pizza

People have eaten bread for thousands of years. Loaves have been found in ancient Egyptian tombs that are over 5,000 years old. Today, there are many kinds of bread from all over the world, and the same dough that is used to make bread can also be used to make pizza.

MAKING DOUGH

Bread dough is usually made from four ingredients – flour, a leavening ingredient, such as yeast, to make it rise, salt and a liquid, such as water. The flour used to make dough usually comes from ground wheat but flour from other grains, such as rye and corn, can also be used.

KNEADING DOUGH

Before baking it to make bread, dough must be kneaded. To knead dough, sprinkle some flour onto your work surface then turn the dough out on to the surface. Using the heel of your hands, press down on the dough to flatten it. Fold the dough over into a ball shape and press it again with the heel of your hand. Continue pressing and folding, trying to end up with the dough in a ball-shape each time. This basic dough can be made into rounds to make pizzas or shaped into loaves or rolls. Extra ingredients, such as dried fruit and herbs, can be added to give the bread a unique flavour.

BREAD FROM AROUND THE WORLD

There are hundreds of different types of bread from around the world. They are made from different combinations of the basic ingredients and are cooked in different ways to produce their unique shape, taste and texture. Classic breads include Indian naan, which is a flattish, oval-shaped bread cooked on a griddle. The Jewish bagel is a ring-shaped roll – the dough is shaped, then boiled or steamed before baking to give it a chewy texture. The French stick is a white, crusty loaf that can be large or small. Caribbean buns are a dense, spicy teabread flavoured with molasses and studded with dried fruit.

GET STARTED!

In this book you can learn to make all kinds of bread and pizza. All the recipes use everyday kitchen equipment, such as knives, spoons, forks and chopping boards. You can see pictures of the different equipment that you may need on page 23. Before you start, check that you have all the equipment that you will need and make a list of any ingredients that you need to buy. Make sure that there is an adult to help you, especially with the recipes that involve using the cooker or oven.

When you have everything you need, make sure all the kitchen surfaces are clean and wash your hands well with soap and water. If you have long hair, tie it back. Always wash raw fruits and vegetables under cold running water before preparing or cooking them. This will help to remove any dirt and germs. Then, put on an apron and get cooking!

Soda bread

Breads leavened using yeast need to be left to rise. This traditional Irish bread uses bicarbonate of soda and cream of tartar instead of yeast, so it can be put straight in the oven.

INGREDIENTS

For 1 loaf:
- 40g butter, plus extra for greasing
- 225g wholemeal flour, plus extra for dusting
- 225g plain white flour
- 1 tsp salt
- 2 tsp bicarbonate of soda
- 2 tsp cream of tartar
- 1 tsp caster sugar
- 175ml milk • 175ml plain yogurt

EXTRA EQUIPMENT

- baking sheet • wire rack
- sieve

Ask an adult to help you use the oven.

1 Preheat the oven to 190°C/375°F/Gas 5. Rub a little butter over the baking sheet to coat it all over.

2 Hold the sieve over a bowl and pour the wholemeal and white flours, salt, bicarbonate of soda and cream of tartar into it. Tap the side of the sieve until the ingredients have fallen into the bowl below.

3 Cut the butter into small pieces, then add them to the flour mixture.

4 Rub the butter into the flour until the mixture looks like breadcrumbs. Stir in the sugar.

5 Make a well in the middle of the flour crumbs. Mix the milk and yogurt together and pour the mixture into the well. Stir to make a soft dough. If the dough is dry, add a dribble more milk. If the mixture is too wet, add a sprinkle more flour.

6 Sprinkle a little flour over your work surface. Turn the dough onto the work surface and shape it into a round.

7 Place the round on a baking sheet and, with a sharp knife, mark a cross in the top of the loaf. Cut quite deep into the dough, but not all the way through.

8 Sprinkle a little more flour over the top of the loaf and put it in the oven. Bake it for about 40 minutes until well risen.

9 When the loaf is cooked, put it on a wire rack to cool. Serve it warm with butter.

IS IT COOKED?

To check if bread is cooked, use oven gloves to take the loaf out of the oven. Holding the loaf in a gloved hand, remove the other glove and tap the base of the loaf. It should sound hollow if it is cooked through. If it is not cooked, put the loaf in the oven for a few more minutes then check it again.

Corn bread

This bread is made using cornmeal. The cornmeal gives the bread a lovely yellow colour and a distinctive taste. Baking power makes this bread rise.

INGREDIENTS

For 1 loaf:
- 4 tbsp sunflower oil, plus extra for greasing
- 175g cornmeal • 115g plain flour
- 1 tbsp caster sugar • ¼ tsp salt
- 1 tbsp baking powder • 2 eggs
- 150ml milk • 125ml plain yogurt

EXTRA EQUIPMENT

- 20cm square cake tin
- metal skewer

Ask an adult to help you use the oven.

1 Preheat the oven to 200°C/400°F/Gas 6. Rub a little oil inside the cake tin, making sure the surfaces are coated all over.

2 Put the cornmeal, flour, sugar, salt and baking powder in a bowl. Mix them together and make a well in the middle of the mixture. Set aside for later.

3 Break the eggs into another bowl and beat them with a fork. Add the yogurt, milk and sunflower oil and stir.

AMAZING MAZE

Cornmeal is made from maize, which is a major crop in the southern states of the United States. Bread made from cornmeal is very popular and is served as an accompaniment to dishes such as fried chicken. It is also used as the base for turkey stuffing.

4 Pour the egg mixture into the well in the cornmeal. Stir the ingredients together, bringing the dry ingredients into the middle of the bowl.

5 Pour the mixture into the tin. Make sure it goes into the corners of the tin. Bake the bread for about 25 minutes until it is firm and golden.

6 To check if the bread is cooked, press a skewer into the middle, then gently pull it out. If it comes out clean, the corn bread is cooked. If there are still crumbs on the skewer, put the bread back in the oven for a few more minutes.

7 When the bread is cooked, remove the tin from the oven and put it on a heatproof surface. Leave the bread to cool in the tin for about 10 minutes.

8 Wearing an oven mitt, run a knife around the inside edges of the tin to loosen the bread. Hold a board on top of the tin and flip over the board and tin. If you lift off the tin, the bread should come out. Cut the bread into wedges and serve them warm.

Wholemeal bread

This recipe is based on the recipe for traditional Grant loaves. It is popular because the dough does not need to be kneaded before it is put into tins.

INGREDIENTS

For 2 loaves:
- oil, for greasing
- 900g wholemeal bread flour
- 2 tsp salt • 800ml warm water
- 7g sachet easy-blend dried yeast
- 2 tsp muscovado sugar

EXTRA EQUIPMENT

- 2 x 2lb loaf tins • sieve
- clear film • wire rack

Ask an adult to help you use the oven.

1 Rub a little oil inside each loaf tin, making sure the surface is thoroughly coated. Put the tins in a warm place.

2 Mix the flour and salt together and sieve them into a bowl. Make a well in the centre of the flour mixture. Put the bowl in a warm place.

3 Pour 150ml of warm water into a measuring jug. Check the temperature by putting your finger in the water. It should feel warm to the touch, but not hot. Sprinkle over the yeast and leave it to stand for 1 minute. Then sprinkle over the sugar, stir and leave to stand for 10 minutes.

YEAST

Yeast is a type of fungus that grows quickly. As it grows it produces bubbles of carbon dioxide, which make the bread rise. The perfect temperature for yeast to grow in is 38°C. As it is killed in temperatures over 60°C, it is important to check that the water is not too hot before mixing it with the yeast.

4 Pour the yeast mixture into the flour. Measure out another 650ml of warm water. Check the temperature, then pour it into the flour. Stir until the dough is well mixed.

5 Divide the mixture between the two tins, flattening it slightly with the back of a spoon.

6 Tear off two pieces of clear film and rub a little oil on each one. Cover each tin and put it in a warm place to rise for about 30 minutes, or until the dough has risen by about one-third.

7 While the bread rises, preheat the oven to 200°C/400°F/Gas 6. When the loaves have risen, bake them for about 40 minutes.

8 Following the panel instructions on page 6, check if the bread is cooked. When cooked, turn the loaves out onto a wire rack and leave them to cool.

Cottage loaf

This traditional English loaf has a distinctive shape. It can be made using white or wholemeal flour and is delicious served warm with Cheddar cheese.

INGREDIENTS

For 1 loaf:
- 575g strong white bread flour, plus extra for dusting
- 7g sachet easy-blend dried yeast
- 1 tsp salt • 350ml warm water
- 1 tbsp sunflower oil, plus extra for oiling

EXTRA EQUIPMENT
- pastry brush • clear film
- baking sheet • kitchen scissors
- wire rack

Ask an adult to help you use the oven.

1 Put the flour, yeast and salt in a large bowl and mix them together. Make a well in the middle of the mixture.

2 Check the temperature of the water – it should feel warm, but not hot. Pour the water into the well in the flour and add the oil. Mix to make a rough dough.

3 Sprinkle a little flour onto your work surface, then knead the dough for about 10 minutes until it is smooth and elastic. If the dough is sticky, sprinkle over a little more flour as you knead.

4 Brush a little sunflower oil inside a clean bowl. Put the dough in the bowl, then brush the top with a little oil. Cover the bowl with clear film and leave it to stand in a warm place for 45 minutes, or until it has doubled in size.

5 When it has risen, punch the dough a couple of times to get rid of the air.

6 Sprinkle your work surface with a little flour and knead the dough for about 2 minutes. Cut off about one-third of the dough and shape both pieces into round balls.

7 Grease a baking sheet then dust it with flour. Put the larger ball on the sheet and brush it with water. Place the second ball on top. Dip two fingers in flour, then press them down into the middle of the two balls to stick them together. Using kitchen scissors, make little snips around the edge of the top ball.

8 Grease some clear film with oil then use it to cover the dough. Leave the dough to rise in a warm place for 40 minutes.

9 About 15 minutes before the end of rising time, preheat the oven to 190°C/375°F/Gas 5. Remove the clear film and sprinkle the loaf with a light dusting of flour.

10 Bake the loaf for about 40 minutes until golden brown, then use oven gloves to place it on a wire rack to cool before serving.

SHAPING LOAVES

Bread dough can be shaped into all kinds of loaves before baking: rings rounds and sticks. Many shapes are specific to countries. In France, the traditional shaped loaf is a baton, or stick. In Italy, there is the flat, dimpled focaccia (see page 14) and the flat, oval or rectangular ciabatta. In regions of Spain and Portugal you will find crusty round loaves.

Garlic focaccia

This is a classic Italian bread. It can be plain or flavoured with herbs, onions or other ingredients such as sundried tomatoes.

INGREDIENTS

For two loaves:
- 500g strong white bread flour, plus extra for dusting
- 7g sachet of easy-blend dried yeast
- 1 tsp salt • 325ml warm water
- 6 tsp olive oil
- sea salt • 3 garlic cloves, chopped

EXTRA EQUIPMENT

- sieve • clear film • rolling pin
- 2 x 25cm cake tins or pizza pans
- wire rack

Ask an adult to help you use the oven.

1 Mix the flour, yeast and salt together, then sieve them into a bowl. Make a well in the middle of the mixture.

2 Check the temperature of the water by putting your finger into it. It should feel just warm, but not hot.

3 Pour the water into the well in the flour and add 3 tsp of olive oil. Stir together to make a soft dough.

THE HOME OF FOCACCIA

Focaccia is particularly associated with Liguria in Italy. This region stretches along the coast in the north-west of the country. Another famous speciality of the region is pesto – a pasta sauce made of basil, pine nuts, garlic and cheese.

4 Sprinkle a little flour over your work surface, then knead the dough for about 10 minutes. If the dough is sticky, continue sprinkling on a little more flour as you work.

5 Wash your hands, then rub a little oil inside a clean bowl. Put the dough inside and pat your oily hands on the dough to make it oily too. Cover the bowl with clear film and leave it to rise in a warm place for 1 hour.

6 When the dough has risen, sprinkle your work surface with a little flour and tip the dough onto it. Press down on the dough to expel some of the air. Divide the dough into two equal pieces, then roll it into two balls. Roll each piece into 25-cm rounds and put them inside cake or pizza tins.

7 Cover the tins with clear film and leave to rise in a warm place for about 30 minutes. Meanwhile, preheat the oven to 200°C/400°F/Gas 6.

8 Uncover the tins and poke the dough with your fingertips to make dimples all over the surface. Drizzle over the rest of the olive oil and sprinkle a little sea salt over each one. Sprinkle over the chopped garlic.

9 Bake for 25–30 minutes until the loaves are golden. When they are cooked, use a spatula to lift the loaves from the tins and transfer them to a wire rack. Serve warm.

Fruity buns

These sweet buns are studded with sultanas. They are delicious when eaten warm.

1 Melt the butter over a low heat then set it aside.

2 Combine the flour, yeast, salt, sugar and cinnamon and sieve them into a clean bowl.

3 Stir the sultanas into the flour mixture. Make a well in the middle of the mixture.

4 Check the temperature of the water. It should feel warm, but not hot. Pour the water and cooled melted butter into the flour mixture.

5 Fold in the ingredients to make a soft dough. If the dough is a little dry, add a drizzle more water. If it is a little sticky, add a sprinkle more flour.

6 Sprinkle flour onto your work surface before kneading the dough for about 10 minutes. It should be smooth and elastic.

7 Brush a little oil inside a bowl and put the dough in it. Then brush the top of the dough with a little oil.

8 Cover the bowl with clear film and leave it in a warm place for 45 minutes. In the meantime, rub a baking sheet with a little oil to grease it.

9 Sprinkle your work surface with flour and knead the dough for a minute. Divide the dough into 12 pieces and roll each piece into a ball.

10 Put the balls on the baking sheet and cover them with a tea towel. Leave them in a warm place for 30 minutes. Preheat the oven to 200°C/400°F/Gas 6.

11 Brush the buns with milk, then bake them for 20 minutes, or until risen and golden.

12 Take the buns out of the oven. Lift them onto a wire rack to cool before serving.

HOT CROSS BUNS

On Good Friday – the Friday before Easter Sunday – Christians eat hot cross buns. The cross on top of these fruity buns reminds Christians of the cross on which Jesus died.

Pizza

This classic cheese and tomato pizza is called a Margarita. Once you have mastered this recipe, you can add different toppings such as spicy sausage, sweetcorn, peppers or tuna.

INGREDIENTS

For 4 pizzas:
- 200g strong white bread flour
- 1 tsp easy-blend dried yeast
- ½ tsp salt
- 125ml warm water
- 1 tbsp olive oil
- 6 tbsp fresh tomato sauce
- 100g grated mozzarella cheese
- ground black pepper

EXTRA EQUIPMENT

- sieve • clear film • rolling pin
- 2 baking sheets

Ask an adult to help you use the oven.

1 Sieve together the flour, yeast and salt. Make a well in the middle of the mixture.

2 Check the temperature of the water by putting your finger into it. It should feel just warm, but not hot.

3 Pour the water into the well and add the oil. Stir together to make a soft dough.

4 Sprinkle a little flour over your work surface, then put the dough on top. Sprinkle a little more flour on top of the dough, then knead it for about 10 minutes until it is smooth and elastic. If the dough is sticky, continue sprinkling on a little more flour as you work.

5 Wash your hands, then rub a little oil inside a clean bowl. Put the dough inside and pat your oily hands on the dough to make that oily, too. Cover the bowl with clear film and put it in a warm place for 1 hour until it has doubled in size.

6 About 15 minutes before the end of rising time, preheat the oven to 220°C/425°C/Gas 7.

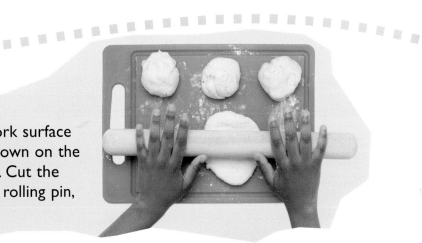

7 Sprinkle a little flour onto the work surface and tip the dough on top. Press down on the dough to get rid of some of the air. Cut the dough into four equal pieces. Using a rolling pin, roll each piece into a 13-cm round.

8 Arrange the rounds on baking sheets. Spread about 1½ tbsp of tomato sauce on top of each one.

PIZZA OVENS

Traditionally pizzas were cooked in wood-fired brick ovens. The ovens were heated until they were very hot and the pizzas were put into the oven and taken out on a long wooden paddle. You can still see this in some pizza restaurants today.

9 Sprinkle cheese on top of each pizza. Put the baking sheets in the oven and bake for 12 minutes until the pizzas are golden and crisp on the edges.

10 Wearing oven gloves, take the baking sheets from the oven and place them on a heatproof surface. When the pizza is cool enough, cut it into slices and serve.

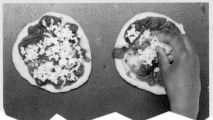

Tasty calzone

When you cut into this calzone, you will find a pizza filling inside the crispy crust. You can use all kinds of pizza fillings inside a calzone – this one has ham, ricotta cheese and tomato.

INGREDIENTS

For 4 calzone:
- 400g strong white bread flour, plus extra for dusting
- 7g sachet easy-blend dried yeast
- 1 tsp salt • 250ml warm water
- 2 tbsp olive oil • 3 ripe tomatoes
- 100g ricotta cheese
- 4 tbsp freshly grated Parmesan cheese
- 85g sliced ham • 8 basil leaves
- black pepper

EXTRA EQUIPMENT

- sieve • clear film • pastry brush
- rolling pin • baking sheet

Ask an adult to help you use the oven.

1 Sieve together the flour, yeast and salt. Make a well in the middle of the flour mixture.

2 Check the temperature of the water. It should feel just warm, but not hot.

3 Pour the water into the well and add the oil. Stir together to make a soft dough.

4 Sprinkle flour over your work surface, then knead the dough for about 10 minutes until it is smooth and elastic. If the dough is sticky, continue sprinkling on a little more flour as you knead.

5 Brush a little oil inside a clean bowl. Put the dough inside and brush a little oil on top of the dough. Cover with clear film and leave it to stand for 1 hour until the dough has doubled in size. After 45 minutes, preheat the oven to 220°C/425°C/Gas 7.

6 In the meantime, make the filling. Slice the tomatoes in half. Press your thumb into the seeds to remove them, then cut out the woody stem and throw it away. Roughly chop the flesh and put it in a bowl.

7 Add the ricotta and Parmesan to the tomatoes. Tear the ham into pieces and add them to the bowl. Tear the basil leaves into pieces and add them to the bowl, too. Add a grinding of black pepper and stir the mixture.

8 Sprinkle flour onto your work surface before pressing down on the dough to get rid of some of the air. Cut the dough into four pieces. Roll each piece into a 20-cm round.

9 Spoon a quarter of the filling onto half of each round, leaving a big border around the edge.

10 Fold over the top of the dough to make a half-moon shape. Press down around the outside and twist the edge of the dough to seal it. Put the calzone on a baking sheet, brush with a little oil and bake for 15 minutes until golden.

11 Wearing oven gloves, remove the baking sheet from the oven and put it on a heatproof surface. Lift each calzone onto a serving plate and serve.

Glossary

accompaniment

Something that is served with a main meal.

carbon dioxide

A colourless gas. Carbon dioxide reacts with leavening ingredients to form bubbles that make dough rise.

fungus

A plant that has no leaves or flowers, which grows on other plants. Mushrooms, toadstools and yeast are all kinds of fungus.

Grant loaves

Traditional wholemeal loaves made by a lady called Doris Grant in the 1940s.

griddle

A metal plate that is heated and cooked on. Drop scones and flatbreads are made on griddles.

hollow

When something is hollow it sounds empty, like there is space inside it.

knead

To pull and stretch dough so that it becomes soft and elastic.

leavening ingredient

The ingredient in baking that makes doughs and batters rise. Yeast, bicarbonate of soda and baking powder are all leavening ingredients.

molasses

A sugary syrup used in baking.

rub in

To work butter into flour using your hands so that the mixture resembles fine breadcrumbs.

speciality

Something for which an area or person is famous. For example, France's speciality bread is the baguette or French stick and Italy's is the ciabatta or focaccia.

traditional

When something is passed down from one generation to the next or is what is usually done.

wood-fired

Heated by burning wood. Traditional pizza ovens are wood-fired.

EXTRA INFORMATION

These abbreviations have been used:
- tbsp – tablespoon • tsp – teaspoon
- ml – millilitre • g – gram • l – litre

To work out where the cooker dial needs to be for high, medium and low heat, count the marks on the dial and divide it by three. The top few are high and the bottom few are low. The in-between ones are medium.

All eggs are medium unless stated

Equipment

ROLLING PIN
Round wooden rolling pins can be used to roll out bread and pizza dough.

WIRE RACK
Breads and cakes should always be cooled on a rack to allow air to circulate underneath.

WOODEN SPOONS
Use these spoons to stir food when cooking or to mix batters and dough when making bread.

MEASURING JUG
Use this to measure liquids and dry ingredients.

CHOPPING BOARDS
Make sure you keep your chopping boards clean. Always use a different one for meat and vegetables.

PASTRY BRUSH
Use this to brush oils and milk onto dough before it is baked.

BAKING TINS
These come in all shapes and sizes so you can bake differently shaped loaves and cakes.

SCALES
Use scales to measure dry and solid ingredients accurately.

METAL SKEWER
Skewers are useful for testing whether bread is baked.

GRATER
Use to grate food such as cheese and carrots. Keep your fingers away from the sharp teeth of the grater.

Index